ASHES OVER ´   T

POEMS BY NATHAN BROWN

GREYSTONE PRESS
2220 N. E. 131ˢᵗ Street
Edmond, Oklahoma 73013

Library of Congress Cataloging-in-Publication Data
Poetry

Library of Congress Catalog Number
2005936417

ISBN: 0-9774576-0-5   Softcover: alk. paper

Cover by Chris Everett
Book design by Mia Blake

Other books by Nathan Brown
Hobson's Choice
Suffer the Little Voices

GREYSTONE PRESS
2220 N. E. 131st Street
Edmond, Oklahoma 73013
2005

ACKNOWLEDGEMENTS

Several of these poems first appeared in the 2005 edition of *The Blue Rock Review*.

To Dr. Gladys Lewis: how does one thank the person who helps him begin a publishing career... You are a saint.

To Robert Con Davis-Undiano: The incredible writers I met while working at *World Literature Today* have had an effect on me that I can't even begin to calculate. Thank you so much, RC.

To David Gross for being "that" professor; the one who lit the fire under my passion for reading; the one who introduced me to some fabulous minds that have affected—and continue to affect—my teaching and creative work.

- - - - - - - -

Thanks to Billy Crockett for being such a good friend all these years and maintaining such a strong interest in what I am up to. Your encouragement along the way, especially at the Okie-Tex Star Party, was invaluable. Onward...

Finally, I would like to thank my parents, Lavonn and Norma Brown. The time, support, love, and concern you maintained throughout twenty years of higher education have been tireless. I'm only now beginning to understand this, because of my daughter. My gratitude is bottomless. You should both receive honorary doctorates in patience.

- - - - - - - -

Sierra – my daughter: You are the measure of my peace and joy, Punkin. You are the "mission" that gives me purpose and strength. So, I offer—as I did last time—the token of dedicating this work to you... *I love you, Honey.*

for
Sierra

TABLE OF CONTENTS

ASHES OVER THE SOUTHWEST

Among the Okie Detritus

Grandma

"Boy—
come on in out from unner that car!
It's time f'r lunch!"

Awed by her ability with language—
and still full from breakfast—
I thought:
Who else could do that,
rattle out five prepositions in a row
without even thinking about it?

I watched oil creep down my hand
and pondered my study in linguistics.
All those textbooks,
and Grandma was still a mystery—
like when I was eight and she
took me out to the garden
through a banging screen door
to show me our "supper, all
growed up outta God's groun',
jus ready f'r the pickin'."

Almost

Didn't think I'd find it, coming back
Highway 9. I wanted to swing by
your old house near the lake, my old
ginger bread hut in the forbidden forest.

I remembered 60th over to Lindsey.
Then, I saw the green street sign—
Flaming Oaks Dr.—draped in limbs,
and it all came back in a dry flash,
body humming, fingers trembling.
From there, the car drove straight to it,
tires crunching thirsty dirt clods.

I felt again the roaring waves of
good ol' Southern Baptist guilt
and the heat from hormonal fires
we tried to put out with gasoline.

I remember climbing through the window
in the silent terror of a teenager,
coming around the edge of your bed,
staring down in unspeakable gratitude
at the threadbare sheet that almost
covered your breasts, knowing
that was all there was
between us.
Your exposed arm and leg—
the moon painting them in milk—
threw my mind into desperate imaginings

of what lay beneath the folds, the lost
and found lines of draping cotton.
I smiled at the cliché of a sleeping princess.
Or maybe you weren't asleep.
Maybe you pretended,
admiring my admiration.

When I finally succumbed,
leaning down to kiss your neck,
your arms wrapped—
eyes still closed—
around my twinging shoulders
in a soft swarm of biology,
dreamily pulling me in
to the pool of your expectant form.

We darted in and out
of dangerous corridors,
danced on mossy graves,
denied that final bliss
from fear of blindness
and divine disappointment.

To get it back.
Just one night.

The ropes that would unravel.

Labor Day

Monday – September 3, 2001

Off work for the holiday,
I decide on a morning walk
in my beautiful nook o' the burbs.
Got to earn that double latte.

Across 48th Street, in a newer part
of the addition—future homes for those
who "want it" more than I do—I hear
Mexicans swinging hammers to 105.5 FM.

Further down, while Anglos check oil
in Lexus SUVs and scold children using
their upper class middle names, I think
of dirt in the creases of already brown hands
as they guide the numbing arc of a trowel.

At the duck pond, while barefooted yuppies
stroll barefooted babies and swing squealing
blond curls in the park, I think of Styrofoam
and black coffee soaking a black moustache
during a wary-eyed break from the sawdust cloud.

Just past the park's Murrah bombing memorial—
a name most Oklahomans can spell now—
while good Baptists wasp their way around
concrete running tracks with Nippon headsets
blasting out a steady American pace,
I catch the explosive echoes of a nail gun
aimed by ojos cansados that wait for el ocaso.

Back at the house, while I slice a peach
onto porcelain and strip for the shower,
I try not to check my skin in the mirror or
think too much about Mexicans building houses.

Momentary Lapse
Saturday – October 20, 2001

I work my way up to the north wall of
        Memorial Stadium,
still on the outside with room to meander.

I draw in the smell of game day,
        unique to sport-loving
minions corralled in titanic numbers.

Getting a head start on throwing down
        trash, white parents
jerk the arms of crying children, because

it's against the rules not to love game day.
        Love it or lose 15 yards,
to be assessed the following play-period.

Inside, the crowd roars like a
        February wave
rolling into Monterey Bay.

Everywhere I turn, I see red
        and white,
and the crowd begins to sing

stars and spangles over our beloved
        Sooners, who were
last year's national champs and still

are undefeated this season at 7 & 0.
        But today
they sing louder than in years past—

louder in a newfound love for an
        injured nation—
louder for the cowboy hat leading it—

louder against pissed-off misanthropes
        who fly 757s
into tall, shiny buildings in a single breath—

even louder against those who sent them,
        in hopes they'll hear
how numbered their angry days are.

Just as they intone "and the rockets
        red glare!"
I glance up to catch the American flag

framed in a massive array
        of ESPN lights,
designed to rob night of its power.

I watch it wave in the Oklahoma winds
        and for a moment,
for a very brief moment, I actually think:

Hell yeah! Kill 'em all!

Chasing Autumn

I'm mapping out this dreamy route
to follow fall throughout the year:

Late summers in Hudson Bay, maybe...
Nome... Reykjavik... a cozy cottage
overlooking the dancing spindrift.
September in St. Brides, Newfoundland.
So fit for a poet—a time zone 30 minutes
off from the rest of the sane world.

I'm thinking Cape Cod or Nantucket
for early October. Maybe Chesapeake Bay
for later in the month. They seem like places
any responsible writer would be caught alive.

Halloween would find me back
in Oklahoma, since I'm sure my daughter
and I will Trick 'r Treat well into her twenties,
and because November here is a stunning scarab
only an Okie knows how to touch
in its yellow, orange, and singing red.

December would be Cozumel or Mazatlán.
Since this solstice is one of two that
permanently trips up the attitude of autumn,
I might as well be on a turquoise-trimmed beach.

I thought about Tierra del Fuego, just above
Cape Horn, for the lead-off month of January.
Any place with the cajones latónes
to call itself the Land of Fire, must have
some latent magic or muse just waiting
to spring on some poor poetic soul.

February would split the trajectory
as I pop back over the equator
to Carmel, California—a mystical haven
for the opposing forces of mountainous,
teeth-gritting waves and languorous fog.
Caffé Cardinale, nestled in a hidden courtyard,
houses two muses—one, invisible, who guides
my pen; the other, quite visible, who whips up
my Mocha au Lait with a sideways smile.

March might work in New Zealand—
home of the amazing bouncing poi balls.
I've only heard of its Tolkien-like beauty
as stoic afternoons give way to ka-
leidoscopic sunsets over the Tasman Sea.

In early April I'll bounce on across
to my own personal legend of Tasmania.
I loved that crazy cartoon on Saturdays
with a nutmeg blur of tornadic fur.

May—Santiago, maybe Buenos Aires,
or Valparaíso, Chile, if only for the name.
June—São Paulo or Asuncion—
each riding on the current flow
or constipation of fickle politics.

In July I'd come home, at least for a week—
you know… to check messages and see
how much money Sierra needs—before
jetting off to Siberia—where I met a girl once
from Kogalym. It means "Doomed Place"—
a longtime curiosity, like the leper colony
of Molokai's lost western shore.

A Note of Thanks

I am terribly grateful to this morning's
low plains snow storm, a Vesuvian
display that floats in so softly, silently
to dust the flatlands with rapturous inactivity.

What command, with a single powdery hand,
to be able to halt all the silly motions
and illusory dreams of commerce.

My own kitchen table, windows onto whiteness,
a cup of tea, a bowl of oats and crunchy toast—
the stuff of an earthly heaven—a river
of love and letters onto these white pages.

Post Script to Yesterday's Poem

By the way—
there is no better spot
to sit with that same
cup of tea,
and read
the
one
word
verses
of Mary Oliver
with all those
foxes
roses
and dogfish in them.

The Twig

The name Jay is what I remember—
witty, hands-in-pockets hallway shuffler
at Norman High our senior year—1983.

We carved out survival in the inevitable clan
of skinny misfits that the puberty gods create
in all high schools to balance out jocks and poms.

Nobody could ever come back on Jay.
Their budding intellects were no match
for his detached scrape of jeans on floor.

But he was so casual about it though
inside his sideways, self-effacing laugh
that always turned his eyes out windows.

Somewhere in the post cap and gown days
some unstoppable shadow overtook him.
A twig snapped in the back of his skull.

The dislodged lobes floated apart
the psychiatrist said, at least that's what
another ex-misfit reported years later.

Jay's just entered the café where I write,
twenty years out from our adjacent lockers.
He walks slowly, cautiously now,

looking for the driftwood of his mind
with his one unglazed eye, nodding
up and down, rolling from side to side.

He sits down a few tables over, pushes
bits of iced cinnamon roll through
a bush of red beard and moustache,

all 300 pounds wrapped up
in a swaddling of thrift coats,
eye out the window…

I miss it too, Jay.
I miss it too.

If I Hadn't Walked,

I never would have known
        the creek falls in a rush
        off the bridge foundation.

I never would have heard
        the scratch of Jay
        claws on mulberry bark;
        the bell-clang of pulleys
        on flagpoles;
        the huffing of a fat
        bulldog running the
        fence for a glimpse.

I never would have thought of
        the breeze's potential
        for peace when it's not
        blowing through open
        car windows.

And I never would have counted
        the ten boxes of Marlboros
        in tangles of dry grass
        all along the way
        and contemplated why
        smokers of Marlboros
        are more prone to littering.

I did see one box of KOOLs…

every study has its flaw.

Donny

I was getting on my mountain bike
in my parents' driveway. His blue pickup
rolled up against the curb—Georgia peach
on the license plate. He'd come from
his parents' house two doors down.

He starts:
Just wanted to say hey.
            Hey, how's it going, Donny?
I'm gettin' divorced.
I couldn't drum up an *I'm sorry*.
He didn't appear to expect it.

He was surprised she'd left him.
I was surprised by his surprise,
but welcomed him to the club.
He seemed to need it.

Shannon's only eight. I'm not
gettin' to see her much.
            Yup, I say. *Those little girls…*
            they'll mess you up.
Yeah.

I miss a lot of what he says at this point.
I flash back to G.I. Joes and yellow helicopters
in fenceless backyards, back before
our parents drew the lines, dividing
play-spaces with chain-link and planks
that we then had to climb over.

It wasn't our parents' fault, though.
Democracy drew the lines for them.
Fences are how we live together, now.

Just like the old lines of marriage—still there
in spite of the fact that every body works now,
no body really *needs* any body, and we've got
millions of other potential mates to choose from,
once this one gets a bit frumpy. Millions of others
have caught on to the workout, trim-down,
tan-line approach to life—the delusional holy grail
of propped up youth and Viagrified sex.

I think back to the time when Donny
struggled with speech problems—
when alligators were "atergators"
and elevators were "aterbators."

And I think of how clearly he speaks
now, of his pain and disappointment.
No misshaped words now…
now that his hair is almost gone,
and what's left is mostly gray.

I'll see you later.
            Alright. Take it easy.

I pull away on my bike,
rolling down the street we'd
lived on all our early lives, thinking
how necessary endings and impending
death are to "living it" this time.

I ride by our old grade school.
Up-side-down children squeal on monkey bars,
holding the bottoms of their shirts up.
Some kick soccer balls at teammates.
Some run without aim. One loiters
alone down among the trees.

That one is me. Poor kid.

I ride past the playground's honeysuckle
scent from yellow and white petals
roasting in the morning sun,
and gasp at the flood of images,
memories—that tiny drop of liquid
on the end of the stamen when plucked,
pulled through and licked, a sweetness
so slight, it's more believed in than tasted.

And now, as I write, I know,
before today's sun sets, I need to go
back to the musty playground,
hang up-side-down from monkey bars,
drink the honeysuckle's nectar and loiter
alone down among the trees.

Another Case for Walking

A snapping turtle, the size of a hubcap,
makes his way under the bridge,
through the shallow rush that ripples
over the corrugation of a drain pipe.
The soupy water glides up and over
his shell like well-stretched Saran Wrap.
He sees me and slowly turns around
wrenching like a ship a million times his size
with the quiet resignation of Eeyore.

Further up the sidewalk, I contribute
to the ever-changing impressionism
of "Smashed Mulberries on Sidewalk"—
a community piece birthed by mostly
unwitting artists unable to savor
the secret wine of the beautiful stain.

I cross the weed-cracked parking lot
of an abandoned Wal-Mart, left
in a wildflower field like a disposable
razor. I cock my head to one side
in contemplation of the ridiculous
reds, yellows, and purples
in petals I crush beneath my feet.
A grackle flushes from a Korean Boxwood
with the pump and pulse of a sprinkler.

As I come up to the side of my café,
I notice a family back by the dumpsters,
mother and grandmother in lawn chairs,
daughter fast-pitching a softball to father.
The daughter screams to the mother
Shut up! Just leave me alone!

The mother, in an astounding moment
of not-getting-it, squeals back in a high-
pitched, obliviously obnoxious voice
I'm only trying to help, honey!

Sports are a bizarre form of child abuse
found mainly in the suburbs.
And I fight the urge to walk up,
shove the mother over backwards
in her cheap-ass lawn chair, lean over
and in a Clint Eastwood rasp say,
I'm only tryin' to help,
honey.

Instead, I step on into the café,
swimming in the buzz, beauty
and anger that flooded my walk,
and choose to immortalize turtles
and bad mothers
and pause to wonder
how it is any poet could,
in good conscience,
own a car.

A Strangely Beautiful Smell of Death

holds my attention
while I search for similies. It's…

like a foggy blanket of second-hand smoke
    that lays to rest closing night clubs
    where you find love you believe will last, or…

like the '84 Monte Carlo burning oil
    in front of you on Main. You know
    the blue-gray cloud is raping your lungs,
    but something about the smell reminds you
    of curbside car maintenance as a teen, your back
    burning on summer pavement while you wrench
    a bolt to change the oil of youth's invincibility, or…

like that steaming daily cup of Mocha au Lait
    that holds your nose above it as you
    reach for the chocolate covered espresso
    beans—each one raking a day
    from the autumn lawn of your life, or…

like diesel fumes dancing in a cabaret
    of Proustian reminiscences about
    high school ski trips and the older girl
    who groped you in the back seat of the Rockies.

Peeling Orange

At six,
she plays with silky scarves
and Gammar's woolen hats.

Orange construction paper flies
from slicing blades to be glued and
slapped onto a larger piece of white.

She staples together unwritten books
from old business stationary,
astounding me with the magnitude
of its previous uselessness.

Leotards and lacy skirts bounce
and dance in the wake of symphonies,
a pristine tribute to innocence
in a blaze of crinkled whiteness,
wiping clean centuries of pure
academic talk about Beethoven.

But soon new school friends
will bring on the parental push-off—
friends denied the bright red
toolbox of childhood's imagination—
and the orange construction paper
will fade even further to brown,
as it's been doing since my childhood.
And Beethoven will morph into
an exposé of belly buttons writhing
on VH-1's "All Belly Buttons,
All the Time" channel.

So, dad writes a poem
destined for the attic

in hopes that someday,
from a certain loss or sadness,
she'll be driven up there
for the sake of sifting, alone,
and crack open this orange journal
that could have stayed blank,
and find these words.

Maybe her tears will fall
into mine, and she'll remember
the orange construction paper
I'm caressing at the moment,
because I've come home.

He Lives Round Here

I barely know him—but enough
to sense the pressure
behind his punctured voice,
barely able to complete a sentence
for fear of its inevitable
lack of coherency.

Something happened back there.
A throat-slit of well-aimed words
cast his eyes to the floor
where they mostly remain,
only occasionally making
efforts to rise and meet you,
as if a memory made of brick
were tied to a hole in each eyelid.

Bleached hair, dressed
all in baggy black, he bounces
behind a musical wall—
head bowed behind
a stack of keyboards,
some salvation train
he believes he's on.

Certain notes, a touch too loud,
are his spasmodic screams back
at the faces of what happened.

Someday, through the scales,
he may even find the key
to the rusted iron door of grace.

Being alive is his ticker-tape parade,
his testament to survival, his hope
for the resurrection of buried eyes.

Price of Admission

Saturday night football game—suspended for fifty minutes at the end of the first quarter because of pouring rain and lightning. Something about goose bumps and raindrops on beautifully tanned shoulders and arms of girls caught by weather—the smell of it all dripping to dirty concrete along with ketchup and mustard over-loaded onto foot-and-a-half-long corndogs. Something about that sudden mid-September drop in temperature that makes you want to wrap your arms around those shivering shoulders—no commit-ment intended—just to… you know… take one for the team. Something about that third quarter interception and runback by the new freshman whose adrenalin speed clips the heels of the storm's lightning, and the fans' rolling thunder that follows. Something about a plastic tray of nachos sacrificed on pavement by a thou-sand shoe soles, then baptized in Coke, leaving only faint traces of sliced jalapeños. I don't know what brings me here. But the corndog alone is worth the price of the ticket I paid too much for on the sidewalk on Asp Avenue, five minutes before kickoff.

S/U – Athlete Evaluations

I am to teach them English.
And I am to evaluate
performance at mid-semester.

Of the three: one listens,
laughs at my jokes, but rides
the razor's edge at "C-"—
a good kid, disarmingly polite;

another is a blow-off,
no notebook in class,
didn't get course packet,
leaves like a prince
out of parliament
to go to the bathroom,
and did fairly well
on the essay exam;

the third sleeps sitting up,
eyes open, never completed
a sentence in his essay,
can't possibly pass
without that great,
smiling social worker
of college athletes:
plagiarism.

And the form reads:
satisfactory=S
unsatisfactory=U
But the law in Oklahoma is:
Love the college football player
aS yoU love yoUrself.

Done

Galileo's on the Paseo.
OKC at midnight.

My brother's band is up
from Texas.
He's mighty fine
on a hybrid blond Telecaster.

Roland plays a five-string
1940s upright Kay bass—
the "Chubby Jackson" model—
eats only organic,
cleanses with special oils
and minerals, smokes
five packs a day.

Local artwork sings
off burnt orange walls.

My kerosene candle throws
shifting arms of light across
these pages while the lost n' lonely
whoop n' clap over Bud Lights,

and I can't tell my brother why
I have no desire whatsoever
to pick up a guitar again
and play in a cover band.

Thinking about Death

lately, I've wondered whether
or not I want a gravesite
for young poets to visit,
leaving prayers and promises
in the cracks of my tombstone
while contemplating the business
of worms.

Grand delusions aside, cremation
seems more my style, scattered
in fourths among the Arbuckles,
Southern Rockies, Sangre de Cristos,
and Big Bend, the four chambers
of my road-worn, vagabond heart.

As in life, so in death…
I want 'em to have a hard time
finding me.

Visitors Guide

Calvin is my town's "paper boy."
He wears a crimson batter's helmet
with a football helmet's mask attached
somehow—a big 36 on the back. He's
on a first name basis, it would appear,
with 100,000 people as he beats
the main drags with his over-the-shoulders
"Norman Transcript" bag. The price
is a quarter. Everyone gives a buck.

He used to be shy in his slowness.
But several years ago, some local-boy-
gone-big made a movie called "Possums"
and based a character on Calvin.
Ever since, he's owned the place.
His twisting monotone has increased
in volume, and he graciously pities
those less fortunate than he, cracking
jokes with businessmen and politicians.

If you visit, take care where one thing
is concerned: *never* touch the helmet.
I watched a transplanted idiot
reach out in faux admiration once.
Three locals grabbed the guy
and jerked him away while Calvin,
arms raised in jaguar defense,
backed out of the café
and down the sidewalk on Main.

I Was There

Friday – July 4, 2003

in red gym shorts and a white T-shirt
pulled up over blue pajama pants.

My little girl, on her bike smothered
in crepe-paper, bows, and flags,
revved an imaginary engine,
her front tire almost touching
the bumper of the police car
that would lead the parade.

4th of July is a simple holiday
for Oklahoma Sooner fans.
Just add blue to whatever
clothes and cars you already have.

I was there for my daughter
who at seven was thoroughly
drunk on the thrill of being
"in" a parade, rather than
watching from the curb.

I was there for my friend, a soldier
serving us well, even though his eyes
are dots at the bottom of two big
question marks—punctuation
on his thoughts about our government.

I was there for my country,
dancing cautiously along in the fever
of maniacal arrogance that builds
to a degree more than hot enough
to burn down Rome a second time.

And I was there for Independence,
liberty, and justice for all concerned
that my president just might be
the most dangerous man in the world.

Lasting Impressions

I. Waitress in Boston:

"So, where's the accent from?"
> *Oklahoma. Where's yours from?*

"What? Well… you're just…a lot nicer
than I thought Oklahomans would be."

II. Yosi, in Jerusalem:

"Are you still having problems
    with the Indians there?"

III. Vitale – Russian Olympic Rugby Player and
        Local Guide in Chimkent, Kazakhstan:

"Amerikanski Cowboyskis!"

IV. Three Israeli Soldiers at the Southern
        Checkpoint into the West Bank:

1 - "Let dem go."
2 - "No no! Dis bad."
3 - "No matter."
1 - "Where from?"
> *Oklahoma.*

1 - "?"
> *Texas?*

2 - "Ma?"
> *Dallas?*

3 - "Oh! Dallas! J Rrrr Ewing! You know?"
> *Yeah… uh… he's my uncle.*

1 - "Let dem go."

V. Waiter at Sam's in San Francisco:

"And, where are you from?"
    Oklahoma.
"Ohmygod."

One Hour

Here where the chrome pin
fits tightly into the very last notch
of the Bible Belt wrapped wide
around the fat belly
of a nation stuffed with
Christians and cock-fighters,
there's hardly a car or pickup
on the streets from 11 to noon
on Sundays—a fabulous time
to go for a walk, catch God
on his cigarette break.

Rockin' Au Pair

So, my friends Andy and Marion
in the band Starlight Mints
are going on tour with Steve Burns,
the Blues Clues guy from my
little girl's favorite PBS kids show.

Apparently, he moonlights
as an angry young pop singer
on weekends away from his
screaming three-foot fans.

Anyway, that's what they'll do
this summer while I hold down
The Opolis Café for 'em…

just the kind of lazy, crazy
thing that happens round here

in my hoppin' home town.

The Four of July

Four of us.
Three have had wives leave
sporadically over the last four years.
One came home to a fiancée in bed
with some other guy.

After the city's fireworks,
we drive south over the South
Canadian River and clear out
the discounted inventory
of a mosquito infested
fireworks stand—
each item a metaphor
for machine guns, howitzers,
grenades, and flame-throwers.

A hippie, a music teacher,
an English teacher, a captain
in the Air Force, all going back
to some beginning on the side
of a dirt road that leads down
to the muddy banks of a patchy
home town river.

The dull red glow of four punks
lights the fuses as we hand-launch
M150s, strings of Black Cats, and
scream variations on *Deya go Bee-atch!*

After years of therapists
and counselors—so many
wasted hours—something flashes

in the pop and crackle of a thousand
tiny fires kindled near the quiet shores
of the soothing, baptismal waters
that flow from God's patience—

"Buried with him...
          raised to walk...
                    in newness of life."

Burn

Oklahoma in July
is a marshmallow
in a bonfire;

a branding iron
on the face;

a toad in the slow-
ly heated pot;

where Fahrenheit
screams until its eyes
turn red—

until the blood
rises in its mercurial veins.

Beautiful and Gorgeous

Two weddings in one day.
Temperature in the hundreds.

The afternoon wedding
in a Catholic church
reverberated in the absence
of a crowd. A friend
from the Frisbee field.
Found by a great girl.
Worked, last I saw,
in the Chick-Fil-A
at the Student Union.
The car with beer-can-
bumper-streamers, filled
with white balloons, was
an old off-white Love
Bug—the big round
53 sticker on each door.

The evening wedding
in the Coles Garden,
outdoors, barely held
the hundreds in attendance.
Two students I'd worked with—
an OU pom girl and a
soccer star—both
as sweet as they can be.
Groomsmen donned expensive
tuxes and Wal-Mart flip-flops
on their feet, like a smart-ass
wink at the toiling masses.
Perfectly can-tanned
limbs flowed from strap-
less dresses, fanning
hundred dollar haircuts.

The get away car—a Lexus. Now,

I wander through the pricey flood
of beer and wine, the multi-
colored buffet with smoked
brisket at the end, and
the Cakes of Gibraltar,
like Bogey in the Casbah,
and think *They're
the same everywhere.*
The poor. The rich.
And the degrees between.

The poor: beautiful, struggling
under the weight of a government
that overlooks them.
The rich: gorgeous, struggling
to overcome tax advantages.

The Watts in L.A. has no
copyright on minimum wage
and desperation.
Greenwich, Connecticut has no
exclusive claim to padded portfolios
and fabulous little teenaged bodies
with all their fabulous little
teenaged made-for-TV problems.

The poor in Oklahoma
are beautiful too.
The rich in Oklahoma,
just as gorgeous.

I Just Wanted to Buy a Magazine

The bottom of my bookstore receipt
is a word puzzle, because
entertainment in my homeland
must never sit, rollover, play dead
for a while, like any dog is intelligent
enough to do. It reads:

blue blue blue blue red red red red r
blue blue blue blue white white whit
blue blue blue blue red red red red r
white white white white white white
red red red red red red red red red r

And I refuse to color it in;
to make a U. S. flag missing
eight of its stripes and all
of its stars,
                          because I'm sick
of a plastic patriotism that carries
Americans about as far and well
as open crates of strawberries,
bananas and blueberries
the length of I-40
in an unrefrigerated truck.

A Defining Dilemma

Just bought the Oxford
English Dictionary on CD-
ROM; Second Edition;
Version 3.0. It cost me
319 dollars and 71 cents.

I look at the box on my table
and think: 900 years of changes
in language; 50 years of collecting them
into this work; and the majority
of entries came from a doctor-
gone-mad-serial-killer the editors
never met but trusted was a scholar
slaving away in a garret—
as opposed to asylum.

But, what's the shock, really,
when one reviews the psycho-saga
of excessive scholarly research?

Sources aside, I wonder
how much I want to know
about words. Will digging in
help me write a more
meaningful poem? Or
will it only lead me farther away
from the sophomore helping dad
bring in the wheat from
the fields north of Watonga,
who takes a short break
on the tractor fender, scratches
his head through a John Deere
hat, and rolls his eyes at this
damn poem the new English
teacher asked the class to read?

Lowland Heretic

Down by the base of a wheat stalk
in the well-tended fields
of lower Great Plains republicans,
I lie
A brown slithering democrat,
narrowly escaping the occasional
blaze of buckshot and boot soles
at cockfights—roosters
with razor blades.

Once buried in the holy waters
of a good southern baptism,
I now raise
a sinful hand up and out
toward the softly shaking head
of St. Jude in hopes he'll rescue
this lonely lost cause
from the rage of a red-faced
denomination that lords an iron
domination over the souls of
good people who can't see the fat
clogging its heart and arteries.

Knowing Better

She sneaks in around 7 a.m.,
slips into the other side
of my bed—angel of seven
years—and we sleep until 8:30.

Her sleep, sound. Mine,
the nervous sleep of a dad
remembering the thoughts
of little nine, ten, and eleven-
year-old boys—punks. They are.
We were. I was. Hormones like
unpopped corn slowly heating in oil.

I give up, shuffle into the kitchen
to pour our juices and consider
having her discreetly followed
by a bodyguard for eleven years.

She follows, a few
minutes later, yawning,
rubbing eyes, still trusting
the world, believing life
might be the rainbows
and pots of gold promised
in her colorful books.

Over cereal she prays
aloud that God will know
we love him and appreciate
the toast with grape jelly.

I pray, lips pressed together,
that God will part the inevitabilities
of time like the Red Sea and drown

all the teenaged boys in our wake,
knowing her prayer is truer than mine,
and that Jesus is smiling at her
with a disapproving eye shot my way.

Found Out

I daydream a lot
about where I'd move
if I could shake this town
and its thick chains:

Paris—until they find out
          I'm American
New York—until they find out
          I'm Oklahoman
Key West—'til they find out
          I'm heterosexual,
each time moving on
when I'm found out.

But maybe moving
isn't what I want. Maybe,
it's going and coming
back again that I love,
visiting all these places
I want to move to until
I find out that their
trashy back alleys
and smelly back doors
of restaurants are the same;
their politicians and lawyers,
rich and poor, beautiful
and ugly are no different;

and that their stupid people
speaking loudly on cell phones
in restaurants are exactly
the same as the stupid people
speaking loudly on cell phones
in the restaurants of my beloved
hometown.

For Some Reason

I watch the 8 p.m. sun
throw shadows from ivy
onto red clay brick just
before summer storm clouds
wrap around the light, as if
they're tired of its heat
bullying us on August nights.

These small atmospheric kindnesses
remind me of the unsolvable
mystery of my love for Oklahoma.

Boston, Carmel... Santa Fe, Colorado
Springs... I'll go any chance I get.
But these places are
the beautiful girl
you're afraid to know
too well, because...

because this is home,
and I'll probably stay
right here
right where
my enemies will always
know they can find me.

Good to Go

I cross the tracks, head past
the front of Sooner Theater
and see Gates ahead of me
in a morning angle of light
through Bradford Pears.

He's got a well-muscled frame
with long, waving blond hair
and taps the thin end of a 3½ foot
tree branch back and forth
in front of his feet, making his way.

On any given Friday or Saturday,
in any given dimly lit night club,
you'll find him playing a mean
upright bass from behind equally
mean looking shades, but
with a smile on his lips about
what some must think is a handicap.

We approach the stoplight at Peters
at the same time. I stop because
of the red light and wonder how
he knows to. I don't hear anything.

I'm about to speak, when the light
changes, and I head out—small talk
never having been a gift. I step up
on the opposite curb and realize
he didn't follow. So, I whip around
in search of appropriateness,
but while I fish, a voice from
the open window of an 80s red Datsun
hollers, *You're good to go, Gates!*

and the stick begins to tap.

Serious Business

Three lines hand-written on printer paper:

> The Diner will be closed
> Aug. 11 – 15
> (Gone Fishin')

taped to the glass door on East Main.
Three disappointed diners chuckle
Yeah, right about the "Gone Fishin'" line,
while they climb back into a shiny SUV.

Eavesdropper that I am, I want to stop,
rap on their window, and say *Oh …*
no, no, no … when Patch says he's
"Gone Fishin'," he damn well means it.

In the Pause

The lights went out
in New York City today,
and I open the blinds
in my house
and look around,
thinking about
what I would eat
out of the fridge
before it goes bad;
how long the pantry
would last me;
how the pecan trees
are dropping;
how beautiful
the night would be.

Critical Care

I caught her out the corner of my eye
and quickly pushed the OPEN DOOR
button to let her in, a grandma trying
to hide the twitch of worry in her cheeks.

Both on our way to the second floor
Critical Care Unit. I jingled keys.
She gripped two huge McDonalds
sacks in one white-knuckled hand.

I, almost forgetting where I was,
almost said, *C'mon Mam, you know
that stuff is why most of us are here;
why it's harder for them to find a vein.*

But she's from a time and place that,
when someone is sick, hurting, and
families are paralyzed with fear,
you go and get them food and drink.

And she's right. And while we feed
the hurting their comfort, McDonalds
feeds doctors their business, and all
have a place in the great circle of life.

Inter-dimensional Thrift Shopping

Two sisters, both with long
graying hair swirled up
in untidy buns with clips.

Two guys, one a ceramic
artist named Sean, the other,
Keel, eats macaroni pie left-handed.

The three not eating, paint Sean's
avant-garde, pre-fired glops
that look like white tossed salads.

The first sister talks of dreams
mingling with reality and butcher
knives mingling with her ex's chest.

And Sean follows with tips
from Buddha and Freud and
some possible mild medications,

never looking up from his fine-
tipped brush, his armpits
darkening from sweat.

The second sister speaks of Jesus
and the time the first sister tried
to kill her in their parents' house.

They had both been so religious.
And the first sister waved it off
and told Sean she'd gone to the

Wiccan place and gotten something
to calm her down, and she
thinks she's doing better now…

And Keel interjects that he'd spent
twenty years stoned, and now
his little boy lives in Colorado,

and his little girl's in Florida
somewhere, and the second sister
immediately steps in with the fact

that the daughter she had not seen
for five years "appeared" next to her
in the thrift store today, and

the girl behind the counter had seen
her too and asked some questions
about her. And a long discussion

ensued with the four around the table
about whether or not this was a good
thing. And the eventual consensus

seemed to be that it was, and that
this was her daughter's way of
bringing their spirits together.

And the sister was so glad,
because she'd bought a couple of
Indian dolls for the apparition—

you know… as a gift, little altars,
in honor of their afternoon of
inter-dimensional thrift-shopping.

The Work of Heaven

Sooner Football kicks off
tomorrow, doubling the size
of our little town—locals
and shop-owners bustling
around like coastal villagers
preparing for a hurricane.

Crimson & Cream flags
line streets, windows, and
car dealerships, and flap
just above the doors of every
Dodge Ram Dooley and
battered Datsun in sight.

And Jubal sounds reveille
as God rolls out of bed,
cracks his knuckles,
and prepares to detail ranks
of jittery angels about the coming
conflict in the prayers of players,
their mothers and grandmothers,
who will be praying against
the mothers and grandmothers
of players on the opposing team,
and how someone must lose,
and how heaven must choose,
and that it's a dirty business,
but, *It is what we get paid for.*

Honestly,

I'm thirty-eight and a half,
and she still packs ice chests
and picnic baskets for my road trips,
right down to the red and white
checkered napkins, plastic-ware.
And I want to tell her I have
money now; I've learned to shop,
don't eat at McDonalds anymore.
But I don't because I love her food.

Here at the tail end of a PhD,
she still follows me to the door
of the house I grew up in, forcing
Ziploc baggies of frozen bread
into my already stuffed hands
while telling me how to know when
things have gone bad in the fridge.
Her face betrays a genuine fear
that I'll eat the expired and die.
And I want to tell her I've had
twenty years of higher ed now
and have finally figured out
the whole mold thing, the smell
of bad meat and bad people.
But I don't because I need the bread
and am pretty sure I ate some-
thing a little funky a few days ago.

I've already lived longer than Christ did,
and I've still gotta eat my veggies
when I have dinner with her and dad.
And I want to tell her longevity
is not one of the hallmarks of my
profession, but I don't because I know

I need the fiber and, besides, nothing
in the universe can stand up to the sheer
force and power of a mother's love.

The Matter of Main Street

I pull past the back
of First Baptist Church
where I was the preacher's kid
for thirty years and park
on the west side of the tracks
under the catalpa tree. My tires
pop and crunch the marble-size
pod seeds on broken up blacktop.

I cross over the tracks on foot
and glance at my milky reflection
in the front windows of the Sooner
Theater, recalling a lip-quivering
performance of one of my high
school garage bands there,
followed, a couple of decades
later, by my little girl's twirling
body in a production of "Bye Bye
Birdie," her eyes exploding
into a galaxy of stars.

Further down, I pop into the bank
that bought my house for me,
pop back out and cross Peters
to the Steppin' Out shoe store
at the bottom of the Vista building
where my ex-wife bought her white
high heels for the wedding.

Next door is dad's office where
he's an interim director of the cool
Baptists—the ones who read books.

So I head on down the sidewalk,
past Bison Witches where I get

cheap beer and sandwiches with
buddies after a game of Frisbee;
past the Midway Barber Shop;

past The Diner, my favorite spot
for pancakes and bacon grease.
Bum's in there laughin' with somebody.

Two more doors down, I wave
at Mack, the always-sharp-dressed
owner of Goodno Jewelry—
dad's favorite golfin' buddy who
sold me the wedding rings.

Then it's around the corner
on Crawford to Opolis Coffee
where Suzie, or Marion, starts
whippin' up my au lait before
I even make it in the door.

We gripe about the president.
Dad and Mack step in to talk about
the latest graphite shaft over lattes,

and I pause to wonder if anyone
in New York or Los Angeles
would ask how my daughter and I
are doing with the recent change.

Holy Cola

On all four corners of 24th and Main,
suburbanites with red SUVs, white
pickups, and their plaid clad children,
unload big blue ice chests and hand out
free Cokes to cars stopped by the light.
Mine is one such car stopped
by their light, windows down
worshipping September.

One of the little boys pops up
at my little girl's window
offering the gift, and she
looks at me for permission—
eyes wide at such good fortune.

I say *Sure, Honey, I guess*,
and when he hands it to her,
he slips in a glossy business-
sized card with it. You see…

I knew the card would come
with it. Because suburbanites
don't just leave easy chairs
without some direct command
from God or Commerce, or worse,
some combination of the Two.

And as I round the corner,
fingering the card that,
as I suspected, was ripping off
the Coca Cola logo to advertise
a local church, my daughter
says *Aren't they the nicest people?*
And I say *Yes, Honey*—choosing

not to follow with the "but"—
the "but" I might follow with
if she were a little older—

But, Honey ... you do understand ...
they're using Coke
*to sell Chri*st.

Since 1955

Don's Alley is over on 29th.
I haven't had one of those
burgers in over a decade.

So I stop in, plant myself
in a deep maroon booth
with a thick wooden table
next to a dark brown stone wall,
all under dim lighting, and I
order the Jumbo Bacon Cheeseburger
with grilled onions, and my waitress
says *Sure thing, honey*, through
a smoker's cough—must a been
workin here since they opened.

I look around. Everybody's
got gray hair n' a gut.
One guy with two canes
orders Chicken Pot Pie
with pinto beans like a benediction
at a brush arbor meetin, and I see

Western art all over the walls,
one painting is an Indian woman
with her child, and I know
the two old farmers at table five
don't give a damn bout no Indians,

and I'm destroyin this burger,
everything I remember it bein,
and I'm thinkin *Man! This is it!*
This is what it's all about. And
I know it's takin a week off
the end of my life, and I'm

thinkin, over the next few years,
I'm comin right back here
and carvin off a few more,

and I know the two old ladies
just come in can barely walk,
but the waitress is spinnin
the third shelf of the Traulsen
window-display dessert-case,
n' she's spinnin it for me,
n' I'm gonna eat that piece
o' pècan pie she's grabbin
no matter what

cause,
I'm just sayin,

Some things're worth dyin for.

Out West

Didn't write a poem yesterday.
Bit disappointed.
I do shoot for one a day, though.
And most of the time it *is* for the simple joy,
       the absolute love of it.

But there *are* times when I do it
for no other reason than
to show those stuff shirts
on the lower east side of Manhattan
with thick scarves swirled around
white necks, on their way
to read at the hippie coffeeshop,

that Oklahoma swims in its own wealth
of crazies, criminals, and the general
insanity that goes with both. And
we read our poems about it all
in hippie coffeeshops too. And
it gets frickin' cold here too
in January, but we don't have to wear
no sissy scarves to make a point about it,

and yet, in continuation of the honesty,
I have to admit—
our crimes do happen in a lower gear;
our crazies walk a little slower;

and I had to look up Manhattan to make sure
it's spelled with all "a's" and two "t's."

I just wish New Yorkers could wrap
their pallid hands around the simple fact
that the cowboys and Indians no longer fight
on horseback. We've moved it into the courts now.

After

I walk in the sigh of evening, the deep breath
that follows the flash of a summer thunder storm.
The sodium orange of sidewalk lights
almost matches the fringe of the cloud line.

Faces appear, as if from a flooded anthill.
Smiles break out in the strangeness of the cool.
Friends, unknown until this vernal moment
greet each other in a sudden camaraderie.

Fins and fishing poles salute each other
in respect to the cycles of life.
Squawking ducks and squealing children
with bread, dance in a circle of giving.

A damp breeze coaxes the smell of beans
and cornbread from an open window.
It mingles with oily pavement
and the must of rain-drenched wood.

Even in the dying light, though,
distant flashes remind me—
clouds will come to storm again
but only to revive the pulse of life.

City of Holy Faith

Quiet Reunion

Just pulled into the town of Holy Faith.
Big clouds promising, but not delivering.
Spanish Market in full swing. Big crowds
delivering, but not promising.

Though Santa Fe is a favorite escape,
I hear an increase in its groans and sighs,

a much heavier stress on its spine
from the profit and decay that always
seep into the most beautiful spaces
when discovered by wealthy tourists.

Along with arriving at the peak of pork
season, with its blinding Hawaiian shirts
and white calves above black socks and
sandals, it's also the tail-end of a bleak year
in which my soul has been holding up
my frail body and embattled spirit.

It is not that I am unhappy to see
my old friend. It's just a quieter reunion
than usual. More like I asked her
not to make any special plans
this time around—no fanfare
or fancy spreads—just time to rest
our tired souls against each other.

I'll bitch & moan about my terrorists.
She'll bitch & moan about her tourists.
And then we'll raise a toast at sunset
on the top floor patio of La Fonda—

To hell with 'em all…

Smacking the Core

The rotting apple core that is
my life these days, followed me
all the way to Santa Fe.

It hovers around my stomach
like an obstinate bee as I sit
in a favorite coffee shop to write,
struggling to endure what has
always been an easy joy.

It plops along behind me
in the thin back alleys, splashing
in putrid, iridescent pools, laughing
at my childish insecurity, smelling
a bit worse with each grungy bath.

It even followed me into
Longevity Café—paradise
on earth, and tried to spoil
my Vietnamese Spring Rolls.

But then, I ordered, in defiance,
the Ginseng Chai Pumpkin Pie
with Soy Dream Ice Cream.

It was as if I had smacked the core
in the middle of its jiggling seeds,
sent it sprawling into the far corner
of the orange and red room.

I ate with avarice. Buena Vista
Social Club crooned on the stereo,
and the core huddled in the corner,
shaking, afraid I would
stride over and smack it again.

On Stopping

I turn around
just before 285 hits I-25.

Looks like an older couple
with a flat on a tiny trailer.

Texas tag, I notice.
The land of my birth might
make for conversation.

She has white hair and spews
a steady stream of small town
drawl into a cell phone. Just like
all the Aunt Doris's I've ever met.

When I get to the trailer, I see
more white hair, a sizeable belly
and black socks with tennis shoes
sprawled underneath.

Need some help?

Boy a' sher do!

That's when I catch it in the corner
of my eye—his aluminum hospital cane
lying on the weed-cracked asphalt.

I dig in with both hands and
let black grease seep into the pores
of my fingers like an easy tattoo.
I help like an English major
with the best of intentions.

Washers and lugs tight,

he works his way out.
A big cut from the gravel
drips down his right arm.
He hoists himself with an adept
cane trick and hobbles to the back
of the massive Cowboy Caddy.

He throws tools into the camper shell
eyeing first the blown tire
leaning against the guardrail,
then the dripping red on his arm.

Briefly missing the message,
I finally offer to throw it
in the back for him.

He thanks me.
She thanks me.
They roll off.

I stopped.
I stopped because there's
hell in my life right now,
and I want God to notice me.

I climb back in the van,
watch my new tattoos wrap
around the steering wheel,
and wonder:

Did that count?
Is that what Jesus waxed
about in the back of Matthew—
something about love

and the least of these?

Well, no Milkbone dropped
from the patchy New Mexican clouds.
And my motives were shameless.

Yet, there is the simple fact:
they needed help,
and
I stopped.

An Okie Mingles

La Plazuela
en La Fonda.

My usual table
in the back corner,
just out of the sunlight.

Enchiladas del Norte
y sangría con una
fresh yellow palm daisy
next to my vaso de agua.

The rough stone floor
slopes toward la mesa
in front of me where
a gray haired madre
y una hija linda
share lonche en paz
and conversation.

La hija is a
magazine cover.
But la madre es
mas bonita a me.

Something she knows,
something viejo,
something that holds
her shoulders back,
and her daughter
en su corazón.

A Palpable Patron

It's tough to maintain
a patron saint
when you've grown up
a Baptist preacher's kid.
But, when you've got one,
you've got one,
Catholic or not.

St. Jude, patron saint
of lost causes—intercessor
of desperate situations—
made himself known to me
over the last couple of years;
came to me knowing I would
not, being a Baptist, come
to him. And I appreciate it.

Turns out, I needed him.

Why should it surprise me, though,
God
reaching over denominational walls.

Protocol

I'm not exactly sure
how this saint thing works
on a technical level.
I just know
that when my
theological questions
grow feathers and
collect like cottonseed
in the air conditioner,
and God feels like he's left
for Latvia because
he needs a break
from Southern Baptists,
it's nice to have someone
to talk to.

Holy Jokes

An old man in Taos once told me
countries and places have patron
saints too. Peru has Joseph. Paris,
Genevieve. But, when he got to

these United States, he said:
Immaculate Conception.
I cocked my head in a question mark,
smiling with only the left corner

of my mouth. I could have sworn
I heard a distant, taunting laughter
echoing all the way from the halls
of Rome—a kick from Italy's boot.

Yes. America, America: a land
gorged on the belief of its own
holy birth; blessed above other
nations; defied on penalty of death.

No room for a humble, humiliated
Christ here among corporate mergers,
ordained politicians, and reincarnated
crusaders against the forces of evil.

Mestizo

U.S.—
east to west, the push;
west European against
the frontier; a frontier
that kept moving west.

THEM—
south to north, the sweep;
the indigenous cut clean
by shiny conquistadores.
Albuquerque *before* Jamestown.
Santa Fe *before* the Mayflower.

WE—
Mexican.   *No.*
Mexican-American.   *Kinda.*
Chicano.   *Maybe.*
            Hispano. Criollo.   *mmm…*

Indian.   *That too.*
Native American…

PDAs & Ponytails

Not feeling overly inspired,
as I'd expect from wandering
the streets of Santa Fe and haunting
some wondermous coffee shops.

But my soul's still weary from the latest
blotch on my karmic rap-sheet.
Just need to sit down for a while.
A rock or log is fine. Just a week or two.

And the City of Holy Faith
idn't a bad place to do it. Profundity
is such a wicked, exhausting game.
And I'd like to give it a rest. Maybe write
to my journal, instead of an audience.

As for "being" a writer?
Don't know why I bother sometimes.
World's got enough of 'em to choke on.

Why ... a "real" one just set up shop
right outside my door, on the patio.
And he's got a laptop, PDA, ponytail,
and chocolate croissant. Now how
am I supposed to compete with that?

With Eyes to See

Santa Fe works hard
to hold on to herself.
Tourists creep down alleys,
through cracks, over walls
like dorky conquistadores—
conquistadorks armed
with cameras and credit,
trying to take the land again.
But Santa Fe is much older
and wiser this time—older
than the landing of pilgrims
in the only three boats American
history high school text books
seem to remember.

I feel the city's eyes watching
this time, arms around its treasures,
wanting to be generous,
knowing the price.

She tries to be patient
with small minds that hack through
entire lifetimes without realizing
bread and wine, stairs and dirt,
can be sacred.

And I want to help her,
though an outsider. So,
I come quietly, tread lightly,
leave   in Faith,
brushing away my tracks.

Flamenco

Well Honey...
it's sort of a...
Spanish Riverdance.

My little girl wants to know
what I'm getting us into
this time.

Oh, she says with weak approval.

But her spongy eyes begin to soak
up the room the second we walk in.
The stage, the lights, the paintings,
the mood.

She sits in my lap, little back shooting
straight up in anticipation. House lights
dim. Black boots begin to pound the wood
of the hollow stage. Her eyes double in
size. A flurry of black clothes and
black hair fling sweat on the front row.
Her hot, moist little palms
squeeze my thumbs white.
A beautiful red dress paints
ruffling circles in flood lights.
I hear a long, whispered,
woooow...

It's late. She falls asleep
at the end of the second hour
from exhaustion.
As I carry her out,
she whispers,
eyes closed,
This is a nice place.

Renovations at the Santuario de Guadalupe

Jesus is on his back
on the grand piano while
workers repaint the santuario.

He's an old, time-worn
piece of wood with chips
on the knees, one on the forehead—
white scabs on one tough man-God.

The painters turn off
the mariachi music on a
white-splattered radio, so we
can discuss sacred images.

And I notice, through the scaffolding,
the nails look as if they go through
his feet, the cross, and into the piano,

and his head, normally bowed
when the cross is upright, looks now
as if he's trying to get up.

Santuario de Chimayó

The tears of last year's prayers,
prayed in this very spot,
well up in my eyes, lids and lashes
like sandbags that can't hold the rising
river. Soaked villagers stand on
muddy hills in my mind and watch
homes and stores fill with brown water,
cars and bicycles twist and wash away.

The prayers for protection and healing were
answered, but now sit like moving boxes
piled in the corners of my heart, abandoned
because of indecision. One by one,
while resting in this rough-hewn pew,
I open boxes and scatter my lack of trust
in God like a panic of doves.

Jesus weeps
and smiles at the same time
in the face of every crucifix
in the sanctuary.

And I smear the dirt
of a miracle on my forehead
and wrists while Christ
wipes my tears with a bloody thumb,
opens his other hand towards the door.

I walk out into a different shade of light,
weak from a baptism few Baptists
could ever understand while standing
in the shadows of their giant crosses
in the giant parking lots of their giant
churches in the suburbs of heaven.

Glorieta

Baptists come, no, they
throng—Catholics come,
Baptists throng—
to their massive, gated hideaway
in the Sangre de Cristo foothills,

chanting creeds built on the cooked
bricks of fear, like any faith,
or cult, that's carved out an
adobe niche in the small valleys
peppering New Mexico's landscape.

They suck the life, bleed the high
desert's water, from the indigenous
they claim to love—much like
the indigenous they claim to love
all around the world and consume
in holy fires like napalm cutting
a path through the hearts of nations.

But here, in retreat, they sing
and sway to the 2% milk fat
of pasteurized praise songs
carefully filtered through the mesh
of dogma by huffing and puffing
old men manning buttons and switches
behind the big curtain—men
to whom no attention
should be paid.

Remember Los Alamos

Best part's the drive in.
The town itself leaves me
a little dry, like every time
my president utters "nuc-u-lar"
for the type of weapons
everyone else should not have.

I'm sure there's something
at its core, something cool
like winter, or a hot nightlife,
but I can't find it.

I turn right on Oppenheimer Rd.
hoping something will explode
into view, but it only goes 100 feet,
then dead ends at the public library.

Sippin' heavy coffee in Café Allegro,
a Peach Granola Muffin just glows
with flavor like there was a great big buttery
meltdown in the back of the kitchen.
A Japanese family sits two tables over—
two fabulous daughters with fabulous tattoos.

The bumper sticker on the register reads:
   Los Alamos
  Birthplace of the Bomb

The trees are all dying in the hills.

Jemez Springs

Think Rain! screams a green sign
nailed to a tree across the road.

I glance back and forth from the sign
to the angry clouds boiling over
the mountains in every direction.

After the last bite of spinach burrito
on the screened-in porch of the Laughing
Lizard, I'm surprised I'm still dry,
the sky having grumbled like a bad
stomach through my entire meal.

But not even the Jemez Thunder
can squeeze a drop to slake
the devastating drought;

just like the Paraclete down the road
couldn't help the problem priests
everyone thought were here to dry out
from addiction to sacramental wine,
but as it turned out, were here because
of a penchant for little altar boys;

just like Father Mac—the one guy
some locals think might have been
trying to heal the situation—
couldn't stop the doped-up maniac
from bludgeoning him to death,
even though he put up a fight,
and even though the maniac claimed
to have been abused—a claim
no one at the time thought to check
against attendance records.

And my eyes come back to the sign
nailed to the tree, and I think about Jesus
and all the priests later released into
the surrounding hills full of little boys…

the very moment my waiter smudges
all my fresh ink with *his* summary:
"Some creepy shit."

But We Want To

We never quite touch,
outside those occasional
light slaps with the backs of
fingers on the other's shoulder,
eyes going wide in a smile,
as if to say *I can't believe
you just said that*! when really
you do,
you do believe it,
and you want to believe
in all and more,
even love.

We never quite kiss,
even in the moment we pause
beneath the acacia in the square,
Christmas lights dangling from branches,
subdued in the distant glow of St. Francis
Cathedral. Not even when our eyes meet,
lock, and linger in desperation,
because we know the ropes
and chains back home will lead
to separate cages like the ends
of every Shakespeare play combined.

We never quite say it,
because words fall like leaves
to the ground and drift away
in the late summer rains
of Santa Fe.

Shits in The Shed

"Poets are shits,"
Tony Mares told me
over Golden Margaritas
at The Shed—told me
that's what his third wife
told him over—quite
possibly—margaritas
when they first met;

this one being the marriage
that has worked the best
for him.

And I thought: *Well … yeah …
I mean … I can't fight her on it.*

But isn't this what pairing up
comes down to? You gotta
pick your shit. Choose one
and go with it.

And I must say,
Tony and I were
two   fine   shits
that night in The Shed.

All the Pretty…

Down on the square
tonight,
they're all beautiful:

unwashed guitar players,
low-rider pimpin' dopes,
the crazies preaching to ions;
even the Guccied-up wealthy.

Hell … even the Baptists
from up the highway
look lovely tonight
in the glow,
the sun low enough to blind
in its reflection off sidewalk bricks
on San Francisco Street.
And even the lady dressed all in black
with a goofy looking black hat that
just paraded through the square
at an angle holding high a long
flagpole with one flag on top—
the Stars and Stripes all in black
and white—and another just below it
with the crossbones of a pirate flag,
but instead of a scull, a frighteningly
good knock-off of George W's mug.

No News Is Good News

Haven't seen a TV in weeks.
It's on at Frankie's in Pecos
this morning, though. And...

well... there's nothin' on it now,
just like there was nothin' on it
that last time I wasted 30 minutes,

because there is no new story:
soldiers in Afghanistan and Iraq
are dying to the tune of two or more

a day and coming down, mysteriously,
with pneumonia in much greater numbers
while Bush, Cheney, and Ashcroft

talk over tea and croissants about
North Korea and the Middle East
somewhere just west of Waco, Texas.

Nirvana at the Coyote Café

I had the house sangria,
the steak burrito—which
has a much longer name
in Spanish—and finished with
chocolate cake, ice cream,
and coffee, all in and on white
porcelain back in the corner
of the upstairs, outdoor patio.

A blue, red, and green, neon-lit
parrot glows like an evil shaman
in the corner to my right.

A street light blazes copper
just over the breast-high wall
to my left, and Christmas lights
are strings of flashing popcorn
on the top floor of the Plaza Mercado
just across Water Street, and I,
upon lifting the last sip of coffee
to my lips while a cool breeze
combs my hair, remember
the one thing
God seems to want most.

So I raise the cup higher
toward heaven first
in a silent toast
before lowering it—
now sanctified—
to my mouth,

knowing
I've honored
the agreement.

Over in the Plaza

I sit on a park bench,
knees tucked into my arms.

The breeze is cool in the wake
of an evening thunderstorm.

The clock on the corner of Palace
and Lincoln glows 10:30,

same time as the night we passed
through the square like two moons

in and out of patchy clouds,
much like the sky's moon does

right now, showing its light
only now and then.

Loud-talkers laugh and screech
over beers on The Ore House balcony.

Two policemen stand, hands in pockets,
on the corner of Lincoln and San Francisco,

and two city workers clear off chairs
in front of the stage across from

the Palace of the Governors, as if
something is over and not coming back.

That's when a couple kisses beneath
the lights strung in the acacia tree,

and that's when I have to leave, because
something is over, and it's not coming back.

Leaving Longevity

Yellow floodlight
and lazy drizzle
glaze the red brick patio
just outside my window.

The usual muffled frenzy
of hippies left early tonight,
leaving only the easy bass
of the stereo system.

In a quiet goodbye to the muse of
enchantment, I order the Ginseng
Chai Pumpkin Pie with organic
crust and High Desert Honey.

I have to leave Longevity.
Can't afford too much Santa Fe,
its Holy Faith of excess creativity
and ambrosia of the Lotus Way.

Besides, my publisher
couldn't possibly afford to print
four books of poetry a year.

On Returning

I sneaked back into town
one more time this morning
before hitting 285 to 40.

Café Pink. Roger and Annie
have fixed me up for the road
with a mocha au lait and scone.

It's in the upper 60s here
at my patio table. I'm soaking
in it before the 103° of home.

Yes… an eight hour drive
can raise you 43 degrees
in the southwestern summers.

They tell me to pop back over
in early October for the leaves
and quiet. I think I'll oblige.

Texas Almost Touches Colorado

Road to Nineveh

A favorite way to flee
the religious filibuster
that is the state of Oklahoma
is to hit I-35 South to that
material Emerald City
in the north of Texas where
Dorothy's house bounced
on the unsuspecting witch.

As I blow down the inside lane
and cross the Red River—
tainted by Moses' divine dipstick—

I see a mighty storm blowing,
racing up behind me, so I
quickly move over to let it pass—
a preacher's wife in a nutshell brown Caddy,
late for a Friday evenin' potluck,
designed to keep men out of bars.

There's just enough time to read
the license plate—"PRAISEM."
I toy with the grammar
'til I get lost in Denton.
I make a U-turn at Scripture Street.

Finally, in Oz, I successfully navigate
the corner of Beltline and Preston—
America's most dangerous intersection.
So says my most dangerous friend.

Now, at his house, we settle into cushions.
And no matter how much wine and cheese,
no matter how much I love to hate religion,
our talk often turns, eventually, to God.

Perdition

I sat on a beautiful lawn chair
on the beautiful back porch
overlooking the beautiful pool
of the beautiful home
of my beautiful friends
in a suburb of

Dallas.

And, all the while,
the incessant growling,
hacking and coughing
of an industrial-sized
Ashplund tree mulcher roared
and sprayed its wooden sputum
into the back of a diesel-humming
orange and black truck
like some sick, anachronistic,
metal mastodon—

as if the twenty first century
needed to add a new circle
to Dante's raging hell
in order to keep up with
the magnitude and volume
of its planet-sodomizing sins.

My friends are moving to the Hill Country.

Happyness

The First Baptist Church of

    Happy,
               Texas

burned to the ground
not long after a tornado
had blown its roof off.

        hmm…

Elemental

There is a place I know
where the air around the cedars
heals the heart of its arrow wounds;

a space I've kneeled in
and felt the foot of greed
lift its heal off the neck of my soul;

where my lungs pull in life
filtered through the blood
and sand of these Texas hills;

where the fingers of my mind
relax their grip on the illusion
of answers and absolutes;

where the fire of creation burns,
and the rock of art's necessity stands,
a memorial, midstream in the waters.

The Quiet House

Deep among the cedars
in the hill country of Texas,
overlooking a deep canyon
stream that feeds the Blanco,
there is a cabin with front
and back porches as big
as its inside. Big as its heart.

Hewn wood and crafted stone
dance in a peaceful revolution
among nature, leaving deer
indifferent to its presence.

When I honor its code
I can almost hear the ants
marching down the counter;
the conversations of ghosts
among the burial mounds.

And when the steaks are grilled
to perfection, the cabernet
poured to the brim,
and the breeze perfumes it all
through the frayed trunks
of cedars, time diverts
into an easy flow
of dreams in the night
that will make tomorrow's
day an easy return.

Where I Go

A quiet angel sits
on the southern rim
of a lonely overlook,

a hidden guardian
among the blue
rock and cedars.

She offers rest

to the singer
whose song wilts
in the heat
of an earless audience

to the painter
whose brush hardens
in the primary colors
of market demands

to the poet
whose prophecies
bounce off the doors
of a dying church.

San Marcos

The grit and hipness in this town
stares you down like the glowing tips
of cigarettes between every first
and second finger of every hand
in The Coffee Pot, where I sit
by the window looking out across
the street at Lady Justice holding
the scales atop the courthouse,
suffocating in a thick glaze of silver
like a cheap version of the girl in *Goldfinger*,
like the cloud around the girl in front of me
with her head tilted towards textbooks,
but like, talkin' on her cell phone, like
she's not too young to be, like, smoking
and, like, drinking coffee, you know?

And I wonder if her dad's a cowboy
like the bronze statue of a horseman
there on the corner of LBJ & Hopkins
who through the haze in this place appears
to have smoke pourin' from the barrel
of his pistol pointed up at the big Texas sky
as if to say *Don't come down here … don't
even pass through these here parts…
unless yer serious, ya' damn Okie."*

Highway 24

I cut through the heart
of Colorado today.
Highway 24,
cheesecake of America:
thick sliceable frosting
        of layered snow,
atop a black forest filling
        of spruce and pine
with a rich brown needle crust,

nature's way of fighting to keep
the fundamentalist hordes
that have flocked to this state
home from Sunday school.

I zipped right by
a roadside marquee
that jerked my neck
back for a second:

"Revival Canceled"

Simile

/'sImIlI/ *n.* 1. esp. poetical comparison of one thing with another using
the words 'like' or 'as' (e.g. *as brave as a lion*). 2 use of this.
[Latin, neuter of *similes* like]
— The Oxford Dictionary of Current English

I've been trying to think of a simile
that would do justice to

that slow drive home
after that storybook first date
where your arms occasionally bump—
because you're wanting to touch
but are afraid of being overt—
while walking over the bridges
of a gaspingly romantic town,
like Manitou Springs or something,
and the fact that this is not a good time
in your life to be feeling this way
makes your heart pound against
the wall of practicality even harder
because you know…
    you know…
        you're sunk,

and all I can come up with is—
it feels a lot like

that slow drive home
after that storybook first date
where your arms occasionally bump—
because you're wanting to touch
but are afraid of being overt—
while walking over the bridges
of a gaspingly romantic town,
like Manitou Springs or something,

and the fact that this is not a good time
in your life to be feeling this way
makes your heart pound against
the wall of practicality even harder
because you know…
   you know…
      you're sunk.

Necessities

Weatherman told
of the coming storm.
This very afternoon
Denver could see more
snow than its ever seen.
The Springs could get
two to three feet.

We made plans.
Little yellow stick 'em lists
multiplied into confetti
throughout the cabin:
bread, bacon, and marshmallows;
kindling and logs;
jugs of spring water;
park the car down the hill.

Mountain Survival 101.

Then it hit mom
in a flash of panic—
"Books!
We must get to the
Book Broker downtown!"
How fortunate the wine shop
was right on the way.
Barely enough time
for groceries and firewood
on the way back.

Deficit

Over coffee
at Pikes Perk,
the one who *is*
Spanish—
looks
Spanish,
speaks only
Spanish—
stoically dries tears
of boredom before
they leak out,
fingering his mug,
eyes on floor,
then the door.

The one who is *not*
Spanish—
does not look
Spanish,
mixes English with
Spanish—
is patronizingly proud
of his limited
Spanish   which
he's obviously working on
to communicate better
with employees who are
Spanish   and,
of course,
out of his deep appreciation
for the exchange rate between
the peso and the dollar.

Again

"The vision of Christ that thou dost see
Is my Visions Greatest Enemy ...
Both read the Bible day & night
But thou readst black where I read white"
— William Blake

Wrestling always with when
to speak and when not to.
Wondering if I'm wrong.
My uncertainties no match
for their absolutes. My freedoms
no match for their creeds
and doctrines that scream
This is it! at every corner
in every town of this nation.
The Pharisees are alive and well
and flocking to Colorado.

Yet, even in my uncertainty, I shout
from the rocky foothills my protest,
scream from the gutters *Yes!*
You're right! Jesus is coming again!
And he'll be just as pissed
as he was the first time,
and he'll throw your welcome tables,
piled with propaganda and tracts,
just as far as those of the money-changers!

And I'll be thrown into anonymity,
metaphorically beheaded, sentenced
to the dungeons of Dobson's *Focus*
on the Family in the Springs—
the New Jerusalem—and my head,
rolling on its shiny floors, will still
be yelling about the rape of scripture

until Jesus does return to put a finger
to my lips, letting me know in the glow
of heaven's eyes, he'll take it from here…

again.

United States

Except for the thin membrane
of Oklahoma's Panhandle,
Texas and Colorado almost touch.
On a clear day one could almost see
smoke signals from the other
drift up and over Black Mesa,
where jackrabbits jet among sage.

There is something of the in-between
in this windblown space where
my four favorite states hold hands
in a delicate agreement—
not quite trusting each other,
but trusting "all else" much less.

There is a quiet hill here that
never forgot the Trojan War,
the Fall of Rome, or the Spanish
Inquisition, because it never
knew they happened.

There is a small town here, Boise
City, that knows World War II,
because in '43 a home team B-17
mistook the courthouse lights
for a test range down the road.

Here where Texas almost
touches Colorado, the rocks
and stunted trees stand
between states, between
generations, between galaxies.

This place laughed the day
the power-grid shut down
in New York City—snorted
at their panic and shock.
This place where I first saw
the rings of Saturn through
a friend's eight-foot telescope
at the Okie-Tex Star Party.